It Must Have Been A Sunday

Catherine Benson

Smith/Doorstop Books

Published 2005
Smith/Doorstop Books
The Poetry Business
The Studio
Byram Arcade
Westgate
Huddersfield HD1 1ND

Copyright © Catherine Benson 2005
All Rights Reserved

ISBN 1-902382-79-X
Typeset at The Poetry Business
Printed by Swiftprint, Huddersfield
Reprinted 2008

The Poetry Business gratefully acknowledges the help of Arts Council England and Kirklees Metropolitan Council.

Acknowledgements
Many thanks to the editors of the following, in which some of these poems first appeared: *Eating Your Cake…And Having It* (Fatchance Press), *The North, Rhyme & Reason, The Spectator, Spirit of Bradford* (Redbeck Press), *Through* (Wellhouse Publications).

Catherine Benson spent most of her childhood in Scotland and now lives in Bradford. When she left teaching she began illustrating and writing. She has poems for children in many anthologies. Under the name Cathy Benson she has illustrated two recent children's books: *To Catch An Elephant* and *Omba Bolomba* (written by Gerard Benson and published by Smith/Doorstop Books).

This is her first collection for adults.

CONTENTS

5	Saturday Night 1942
6	49 Clyde Street
8	The Widow
9	Ex WRNS Shoes
10	Invergordon: Denial
11	The Tailoress
12	At the Mortuary
13	Lynn
17	My English Grandfather
19	The Scythe
20	Weekend
21	Garlic
22	Bradford Allotments January 1st
24	Going for the Newspaper
25	This Woman
26	On Looking at a Lightswitch
27	Genes
28	At the Bus Stop by St Iowan's, Llanystumdwy
29	Cormorants
29	A Crow on a Winter Birdtable
30	Wing Bone
31	Snapshot at Foldøy
32	Fairy Tale

for Gerard with love

SATURDAY NIGHT 1942

On Monday she saw it in the Co-op window.
All day it shimmered in her eyes.
The week's work was softened by its folds;
Friday's pay, savings and coupons handed over.
Next week's hunger was the small print
she didn't read on the receipt.

Saturday, the dance and dreams,
the stuff her living's made of.
Her pal is green about the dress; says,
'It's maybe a wee bit *tight* about the breast.'
But, the band plays.
Their legs are up and away to the floor
all girls together, what with the war.
The few locals at the bar wait the beer's go-ahead

The singer from down south sings U.S. drawl.
In a few weeks G.I.s will sing it for real.

The drums syncopate her blood.
The song closes her eyes. The sax drives her hips.
Her flame silk dress slides to the rhythm inside.
The beads at the hem sashay four-four time.

Errol Flynn, dinner for two, moonlight and magic,
black satin sheets: poor melancholy baby.
She isn't misbehaving, she's saving all her love.
Behind her lids the Silver Screen rolls by.

.

49 CLYDE STREET

Gold blossom on the red tree
on the black tea caddy rivals
the brass candlesticks.

The rhythm of the wooden clock
is absorbed into heart beat.

Tongs reach small hands to the coal bucket.
The poker, bent-backed from hot embers
leans to the leaded range. The fender gleams,
Brasso burnished.

The kettle, as black as the stock pot, puffs
white vapour into grey smoke.
The chimney breathes in.

The rag rug is the outworn clothes
of unknown relatives and family history.

A blue glass rolling pin, painted
with flowers hangs on a cord, too grand
for the making of pastry. Its cousin,
of scrubbed wood, lies in a drawer.

Grandad looks down from the opposite wall,
in uniform, austere in his moustache,
'The best man that ever lived,' says Gran.

Close by, his ship ploughs a heavy swell
in a rectangular world of black and white.

The sideboard hoards the best china.
The piano waits for Saturday nights.

In the scullery the washboard rests
until Monday and socks and collars.

In between there is Sunday
and a white cloth over the chenille of the table
and high tea, rent permitting.

The window shuts out the cold, but sliding in
on a draught, the bakery opposite rouses
the nose and the taste buds (ah! butteries!)

The back yard is lavvy, washing line,
coal bunker and hopscotch. Over the wall
is someone's garden – with pear trees.

Forty-nine on the front door dazzles the sun,
the step is laundered. The whole street
knows Mrs MacKenzie and her granddaughters – us.

THE WIDOW

'The Black Wifie' rarely went out of her door,
did polish its brass, scrub its step.
The only colour she wore was on her apron.

There was always a kettle on the stove,
always a fire and a 'Come away in'.
If the baking tin was empty, time was food enough.

Time, she had for everyone. It was a rich house
though it was porridge or soup on the table.

Tinkers called for hot water and a twist of tea.
The minister called for a warm up (sorely needed).
She had little to put in his brown envelopes
but she put it.

When she became bedridden he forgot to call.

Crippled from childhood she would still
tap her feet to our dancing, sang pop songs,
could yodel.

*

In the nip of her nose
she used to say she could smell snow.

In the stiff board of sheets from the line
she declared it was too cold for snow.

Predicting power cuts in the rising wind
she trimmed the oil lamp.

Sunshine to 'make hay' by
was for others and health for the bairns.

She went no further than her own doorstep.

EX WRNS SHOES

She said they were a bargain.
She'd worked at the hospital during the war,
never been a Wren. Yes,
she would have liked to have been.

He mended them on his last, cut leather
paring it like an apple to fit heel or sole.
I polished them, a black buttering
that I rubbed to a shining of wet coal.

And, just for love, I polished the instep
careful not to mar the creamy sole,
inhaled its pungent newness,
admired the neat border of tiny nails.

She would walk me home to my grandmother's
or, to visit my aunt in Saltburn, more than a mile,
marvelling at their comfort. 'Like new…' she'd say.
They were a bargain.

He was a bargain too, the things he could do.
She said he could turn his hand to anything.
And she? She made sure he was looked after;
meals on time, cooked just as he liked them;

given the newspaper first to read, given
quiet for his football on the radio.
She gave him his position – man of the house.
When we didn't know something we'd ask him.

The soles and heels dirtied, wore out, wore down.
The uppers moulded to her feet, the bunions' bulge.
He mended. I polished.
Standing empty they lean outwards.

INVERGORDON: DENIAL

She did not live with her grandmother,
did not have a mother somewhere else.

She did not go with her grandmother
to talk to her dead grandfather.

The wind was not from the mountains,
was not bitter, was not in her face.

She did not hear those words about
the mother who could come and take her.

She did not kiss her Gran goodbye each day
when she left for school, just in case.

*

Five years later her grandmother did not
stand on the corner of the street

asking when the bairns were coming back,
when the bairns were coming back.

THE TAILORESS

She pulled gold thread through beeswax
to ease its way through gold braid.

Flakes of wax like fudge crumbs
lay in grooves carved by the thread.

Her days were spent sewing promotions on sleeves,
medal ribbons, epaulettes.

Her needle pierced braid and serge
with a fierceness like revenge.

Her nights were spent unpicking her life,
easing its thread through whisky,

crumbs of dreams and what might have been
swept away in black out.

AT THE MORTUARY

Julia

The face I recognised on the trolley
was no longer dangerous. I stood this side
of the safety barrier, she 'slept' on the other,
face to the ceiling, her story finished – the end;
the book of her closed.
I'm sorry I missed the first chapters.
I search the album for clues.

The face I didn't know looks to the left and up.
It does not stare into the camera
where I might read the eyes.
The mouth is a small lipsticked smile,
dark in this black and white snap.
The face is pretty, a stranger's face.
I might have liked her, *if things had been different.*

LYNN

a poem in five parts

1. From the Back of a Cupboard 2001

The doll with broken arms is mine now.
Audrey you called her. I asked you where you got the name.
I don't remember your answer.
I do remember how I coveted the doll
with the last remnants of childhood.
At eleven I was too old for dolls our mother said.
My December birthday had passed with this disappointment
and Christmas brought Audrey to you.
In 1953 she was the latest model,
a doll who walked when you held her hand
and turned her smiling head from side to side
and wore real shoes.

2. Old Photograph

On Sunday afternoons we went for walks.
When I was nine and you were seven we met the dog
that harried us, tore my coat sleeve and your glove.
You buried your head in my chest and cried.

When I was eleven and you were nine
we walked on the dunes, collected lemonade bottles,
golf tees and what we thought lost balls
half buried in the sandy holes behind the dunes.

When I was thirteen and you were eleven
we walked Welsh lanes, looked at churches,
wished we could find a farmhouse, just like in a book,
where there would be a welcome and milk and scones.

When I was fifteen and you were thirteen
we walked apart. We did not know each other.
I tried to hold you but you wriggled free into yourself.
We hardly spoke, you always had somewhere else to be.

I have a snapshot of us walking with our prams,
dolls tucked up, us in coats and woolly hats, posing
in winter sunshine. It must have been a Sunday
because on Sunday afternoons we went for walks.

3. Truant

The summer season spent with beach ponies
turned you honey-brown, bleached your yellow hair.
Careless of looks, not yet in your teens,
you scraped it back and bound it with a rubber band.

Someone had given you old jodhpurs.
You hid them in your satchel where books should be.
Your school thought we'd moved away.
No one came to the house or sent a letter.

I was stopped in the street one day, by your classmate
and then it was I carried your secret.
There was little love at home and you hated your school.
You loved the horses, the freedom of the beach.

My gypsy sister, courageous, grabbing the life you needed.
I hope it was possible without fear.
You were twelve then with only three more summers to see.
I wish I had not told.

4. The Collection

Chinese horses, white-glazed with gilded manes,
gallop, trot or roll over on the chest of drawers;
squat and round-bellied as the beach ponies
you led along the shore of Hayling Island:
your first Saturday job and money for this collection.

Long before that we watched
Saturday morning cowboy films;
watched dust clouds raised each week
by the chase, the escape, the posse.
Afterwards we ran on the Lossiemouth dunes,
the chaser and the chased. We took turns,
the goodie, the baddie, the rescuer, the rescued,
galloping our own story. The shanty town
of beach huts, our Klondyke – gold
in returnable lemonade bottles
pushed into sand under wooden steps.

Three years put childhood games aside.
You escaped from me into your horse-world,
escaped school, and home with its bar-room brawl.
In real life there is no Cavalry.

Jerky frames of memory crank on.
I watch our separate trails, me –
homework, exams, a job, marriage.
And you – horses, always the horses.

They gave me your collection.
I kept them shoe-boxed for years
then gave them to your niece,
my first child, born that year of your last gallop
over an icy Dartford Heath.

Now your grandniece lifts them out
sets them on the floor to gallop, trot,
and roll over: and over and over you
in my mind, your tanned skin, sun-bleached hair,
sand in my eyes.

5. Lynn

1945-1961

Framed by the hospital bed,
the white pillow, the white sheet,
white counterpane all seem a blank canvas.
Only a head painted in,
blonde tendrils curled round a brow yellowed
to the colour of ivory.
Your face unmarked, serene in pre-Raphaelite sleep.

My kiss feels the unyielding skin
beneath my lips, the dead marble sheen.

Where did the hooves kick? They said you were dragged
one foot caught in the stirrup and, words
I could not bear to hear then or echo now,
the other horses galloped over you.
Where are those hoofbeats into soft flesh?
You lie in seeming perfection; only your eyelids,
purple as pansies, swollen as plums, to shock.

MY ENGLISH GRANDFATHER

April 1954

I love this hour of day when thin sunshine
corduroys the bare vegetable plot with shadow
and paints these white walls pale lemon
and spotlights dancing gnats.

There was a gardener once, years back from now,
whose hands pushed beans into crumbling soil,
whose eyes weeded out wiry couch grass root,
whose check slippers stamped-in fruit bushes.

But it was cabbages he preferred to grow
blue-green, rubbery leaves in huge rosettes.
I would pinch the leaves to hear them squeak
and send a thousand whitefly flying.

'Tough enough to sole old boots,' Gran complained.
She preferred roses, dahlias, lupins, gladioli,
hollyhocks, love-in-a-mist, lettuces –
anything but cabbages.

When he hosed them down, the water pittered and drummed
and spattered into mercury-balls that skittered across the surface,
slid down the veins and into each heart.
The white fly lay low.

At this hour of day he would stop and rest,
lean on his spade or sit on the upturned bucket.
He would sing music hall songs, smoke his pipe,
tell me about a cowboy film he'd seen.

Sometimes the big brown spots on the backs of his hands
would bleed. – 'Old age,' he'd say,
'skin's wore out, that's all,' and dab the blood with a shirt cuff.
'Sing another song,' I'd say, not looking.

We fell out over the caterpillars.
'Blamed things,' he said, using cowboy-talk and spitting.
Then he flicked them onto the path and sliced them with his spade.
'That's cruel,' I raged. 'They're butterflies really!'

'Don't I know it!' he said, 'little buggers.'
'Pops!' Gran yelled from the kitchen window. 'Language! Ears!'
'They don't feel it,' he said with a glare at the open window.
'No nerves.' – I was not convinced.

On hot August days a smell hung round the garden.
The outer cabbage leaves were holed and yellowed,
a tattered skirt spread on the ground
over woodlice and slugs.

At this time of year though, everything was a beginning,
the earth hoed, raked and ready.
Stakes joined with string, threaded with milk bottle tops,
were set in rows just above each seed drill.

Behind the shed the uncovered compost heap
of rotting cabbage leaves and kitchen waste
would steam, where he'd dug into it.
'It's a cycle, see?' he'd say.

Down in the cemetery they put roses on his grave.
He told me once, 'If I must have flowers, tell them – cabbage roses.'
At this hour of day, at this time of year, I remember him,
his songs, his hands, his cabbages which my grandmother never cooked.

THE SCYTHE

They give me room in this dark shed, a corner of my own.
Spiders avoid me, mice do not leap me.
My blade teases the flower pots and the broom.

In his hands I am a wicked smile in the grass.
I leer at the innocent daisy, the bold dandelion.
I taste the green salt of a grass sea.
My rhythm is his rhythm.
In my hands he becomes Father Time.

WEEKEND

October blackberries are too soft now
for jam. And the apples
not quite ready to bite.

The conkers though, have polished
their art of seduction
and wink in the grass.

Clouds fray into blue air.
The mere is a mosaic of fell and sky.
Swans cruise on Klimpt water.

White feathers from a moulting
moor themselves to the bank
or float as flotsam to the weir.

The silver birch is down to her last veil:
Salome of the hillside
throwing modesty to the wind.

GARLIC

I choose the plumpest head from the pottery bowl,
the bowl we bought in France eight years ago.
The cloves blush purple through tissue-paper skin,
rounded bottoms in tight white trousers.
I choose the plumpest clove, prise it free.
The skin whispers between my stripping fingers,
a few white flakes fall to the floor.
My thumbnail pierces the flesh, oozing
an orchard, a charcoal fire, meals al fresco,
olive oil dressing, crisp lettuce,
sweet tomatoes, tart lemons, soft bread
set on a table with lantern and wild flowers,
you, barbecuing sardines.

Afterwards we walked along the beach
hoarding the day, the summer, our freedom,
parcelling up our store of memories
for this time of garlic-laced winter stews.
I cut and chop and scrape oily slivers
from sticky fingers and later, in bed, you taste them.
'Mmm – garlic,' you say. 'Remember … '

BRADFORD ALLOTMENTS JANUARY 1ST

We shoulder through the dusk of early afternoon,
the grimy brick of back-to-back Naples Street.
We've a hunger for countryside.

The sky rests on chimney pots.

We're making do with the allotments farmed by Asians
in touch with the soil in a Yorkshire city.

Last year in this village of sheds and plots
divided into beds, you saw a Little Owl in October sunshine.
We watched a cat prowl something under a box.
Goats were penned and cockerels crowed in yards
fenced with old bedsprings and various doors.

And foxes were a nuisance, someone said.

We turn right into Whetley Lane and right again
into Jarratt Street. The wrought iron gates stand open.
We straddle mud, wish for stouter shoes,
concentrate past puddles, look up –

smashed greenhouses and lean-tos,
rain-sodden charred remains of sheds.

We walk the aisles between old door-fences.
Here and there muddied plush carpet and cracked lino
pave the path – and everywhere nature
is reclaiming, softening the scars.
Birdsong is insistent, territory is territory.

Back now up Naples Street, wanting
some sight to soothe the bruise of blight.
 Number 27, white door a beacon.

Concrete yard, buttercup milk crate, green wheelie bin,
lilac drainpipe, vine of clothes line,
pin-striped peg bag open-mouthed
and beside it the white door blooms
with a stained-glass rose.

GOING FOR THE NEWSPAPER

Footwear for me – walking boots,
ankle-padded, air-cushioned soles,

warmth and safety, to crunch powdered pavements,
toecaps heaped white.

Footwear for a winter butterfly,
red and green sequins on gold;

dainty heels pierce the snow,
bare toes blueing beneath brown.

We meet halfway on the hill,
smile hellos. I say, 'It's lovely isn't it?'

She says, 'Yes, but very cold.'
Her sari sings of the south, my coat of the north.

But it's East and West who meet on Naples Street,
in Bradford 8 on Tuesday, February '96.

Her cold feet in slipping sandals stop my breath.
Her eyes pity my clumsy clomping comfort.

Tonight I will make curry.

THIS WOMAN

Halfway to town there's a pie and cake factory.
When it blows from the south-east
I can smell my Aunt's baking days.
I know a woman who works there,
skin as pale as uncooked pastry.

She's bled by her husband,
thin, squeezed by living on dread.
Her eyes are carbonised resentment
black as burnt currants in sticky buns.

Her life is meagre, spiked by tragedy:
sugar, spice and all things nice on the top shelf

out of reach.

It's a slow oven, her home life;
shrivels the world to between four walls;
when he's in a stupor
she lives a little, breathes.
She thinks her work is … O.K.

Hates pies.

When the wind blows from the south-east
I can smell her despair,
prefer to flip back to my Aunt, her cakes,
warm jam, blackberry pies, plump home. Only
I know this woman.

ON LOOKING AT A LIGHTSWITCH

We did not have on our wall, a white
three inches square plastic, twin-screwed
to cream plasterwork, twin-switched switch.

Our switch was round brass and glowed in its polish
among the leaves and flowers of wallpaper,
performing the same miracle;

a click and the room lit to every corner
not like the oil lamp's circle leaving dark shadows
which might move closer, become something.

Gran trusted the oil lamp, she'd filled it herself,
trimmed the wick, cleaned the globe and glass chimney.
Its brass base reflected a distorted room.

Each winter night she made it ready, waited
for high winds and snowfall to prove her point;
the power cut.

I longed to grow enough to reach that switch
and with one finger release its magic from wall
to dangling bulb in its parchment shade.

GENES

The glass
on the wall showed
my mother's face so I
dyed my hair beacon red. Still she
looks out.

AT THE BUS STOP BY ST IOWAN'S, LLANYSTUMDWY

Clouds have stopped the sundial.
Church bells are silent.
Headstones give little away,
only telling time passed.
Stones in the wall wear
fob watches of lichen and moss
but tell the seasons, not the hours.

Celandines say it's spring.
A breeze that fingers my neck
says it's winter.
Upturned chairs on tables at the café
mean summer's a long way off.
Brown leaves that clog a drain
say autumn's been this way.

Sheep, head down, think it's time to eat.
The Dwyfor river shouts, Time is only an idea!
A dandelion in the grass verge
is not old enough to give an opinion.
The timetable says I still
have another seventeen minutes to wait.

CORMORANTS

hang themselves out to dry
on the wind.
Heraldic on metalled water
they are gateways to myths.

A CROW ON A WINTER BIRDTABLE

A Richard the Third of a bird,
who struts on a stage of snow.
Theatrical in dress, he silhouettes a pose,
stands head atilt, ebony legs astride.
Breeze-fingered feathers lift about his neck.
He cocks his eye at the bits of food, chooses a piece
of peel from the mixed dry-fruit, a bead of orange, held up
as if he'd won a prize.

WING BONE

In the glass case a Viking flute,
In the Viking flute a secret song,
In the secret song the music of a bone,
In the music of a bone the singing of a wing,
In the singing of a wing the silence of a swan.

(This flute made from a wing bone of a mute swan is in the Viking Museum at York.)

SNAPSHOT AT FOLDØY

He does not look about him,
the man who has just left the ferry.
He is not amazed, does not photograph the view.
He walks a well-known path
between boulders humped huge in withered scrub.
Wooden houses squeeze where they can
between these gigantic stones rolled, ground smooth,
then dumped in a glacier's retreat.
The houses squat, mustard-yellow,
sage-green, rust-red and eye-watering white.
The man walks his path in all weathers.
As season nudges season, he works, he returns home.
The ferry takes him to the mainland and back.
To what work? – It requires that grey suit.
To what home? – It lies out of sight
round that bend bordered by boulders
that lie in scrubland painted by autumn.

FAIRY TALE

(from an overheard remark)

Once a thread's through the eye of a needle
there's no room for a camel.
He must find his own in the haystack
being careful not to wake Boy Blue
who will otherwise cry buckets
at the interruption of his dream about Bo Peep,
to whom he has lost his heart
whilst she has lost nothing more than her sheep.
They, in fact, are in the company of Baa-Baa
who is to be found frisking down the lane
with a Raggle-Taggle gipsy boy who will be glad
to line his rough ditch-bed with the warm
black wool. At night he will lie wrapped
in woollen darkness seen only by the moon
as she ducks under a jumping cow
whose crumpled horn pierces the Milky Way
sending milk-stars down to the forlorn maiden
who will smile and sew them onto her dress
with that needle and thread,
and who will, of course, live happily ever after.